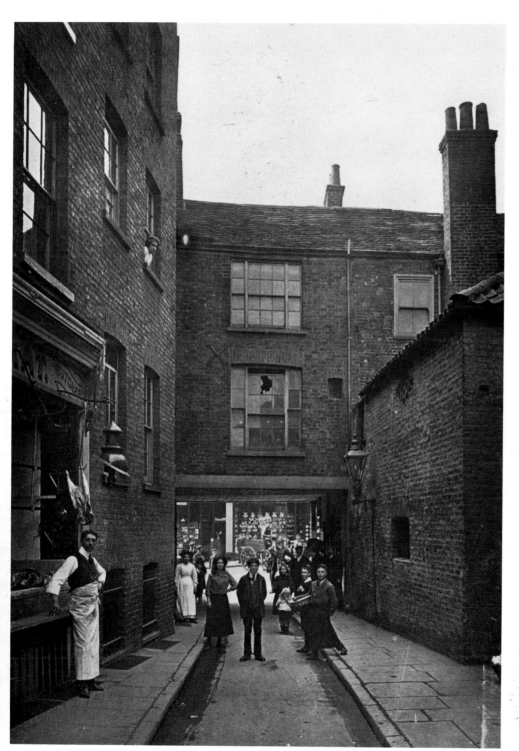

A Pictorial Record

Flask Walk as it was in 1902, showing the two-storey building over the opening into the High Street. This building was demolished in 1911. Below: As it is today.

Right: Heath Street about 1920, looking towards the Baptist Church. The Horse and Groom is on the right. Below: As it is today.

Left: Heath Street from Church Row, looking towards the junction with High Street, 1905. Above: As it is today.

High Street from the junction with Heath Street, looking towards Rosslyn Hill, 1905. Inset: As it is today.

High Street, looking towards Rosslyn Hill, in 1902. The large building on the right at the corner of Prince Arthur Road was a Wesleyan Chapel, demolished in 1935.

Well Walk, 1904.

HAMPSTEAD BREWERY,
HIGH STREET, HAMPSTEAD.

TELEPHONE No. 435.   POST OFFICE, HAMPSTEAD.

LIST OF PRICES.

CASK.			Per Kild 18 Galls.	Per Firkin, 9 Galls.	Per Pin, 4½ Galls.
Bitter Ale	...	AK	16/6	8/3	4/2
Do. Superior	...	AKA	18/6	9/3	4/8
Do. Extra	...	XX	22/6	11/3	5/8
India Pale Ale	...	IPA	25/6	12/9	6/5
Do. do. (Burton)	...	IPA	30/6	15/3	...
Mild Ale	...	X	16/6	8/3	4/2
Do.	...	XX	18/6	9/3	4/8
Do.	...	XXX	25/6	12/9	6/5
Strong Ale (Burton)	...	XXXX	30/6	15/3	...
Porter	...		18/6	9/3	4/8
Single Stout	...		22/6	11/3	5/8
Double Stout	...		25/6	12/9	6/5
Ginger Beer	...	...	...	...	3/6

TERMS : Cash on Delivery ; subject to a discount on Cask of 1/- per Kilderkin ; 6d. per Firkin ; and 3d. per Pin.

BOTTLED ALE AND STOUT at 2/2 per dozen.
(Half-dozens Supplied if required).

Beer supplied in One Gallon Screw-Stoppered Jars
for Cash on Delivery.

Bitter Ale	...	...	1/1	Burton Ale	...	...	1/5
Mild Ale	...	...	1/1	Porter	...	...	1/1
Pale Ale	...	...	1/5	Single Stout	...	...	1/3
		Double Stout	...	1/5			

GINGER BEER in Screw Stoppered Gallon Jars at 10d. each.

Price Lists of Wines and Spirits on Application.

High Street, c. 1914. The Hampstead Brewery sign can be seen centre. Left: This advertisement appeared in the Hampstead and Highgate Express in 1907. The brewery was in business from 1720 until 1921.

High Street in 1903, looking towards Holly Hill. The Bird in Hand public house, on the right, was where the London omnibuses completed their journey. It is now called the Dome.

Haverstock Hill, near the junction with Prince of Wales Road, 1903. The church on the corner was the Oxenden Presbyterian Church, built in 1877. It was acquired in 1970 by the Seventh Day Adventist Church and was re-opened in January 1972.

Haverstock Hill in 1906. The George public house is on the left.

Rosslyn Hill from Downshire Hill, 1905.

East Heath Road, with Squires Mount on right, 1904. Above, left: As it is today. Above, right: East Heath Road, looking towards South End Road, 1906. The cyclists sensibly decided to walk up the hill.

Above: Horse-drawn cabs wait outside Hampstead Heath Station, c. 1904. Right: South End Road, about 1903. The domed building was the waterworks engine house which pumped water from a wellshaft sunk in 1847. It was demolished in 1907. Below: Pond Street in 1905, showing the entrance to the Hampstead General Hospital which was replaced by the Royal Free Hospital in 1974. Below, right: Watching the ladies bathing in the pond, Hampstead Heath, c. 1904.

South End Road from Hampstead Heath Station, 1905. Inset: As it is today. Rumbold's has survived, including the original shop front.

"CANADIAN SCENES" at HEALTHY, HAPPY HAMPSTEAD

Tobogganing from Parliament Hill. — Showing Crowd at the top.

Hampstead Heath Station in its heyday in 1905. The Station, which opened on January 2, 1860, was the scene of a disaster in 1892. The Easter Bank Holiday brought the usual crowds to the Heath for the fun fair. Then heavy rain forced many to dash for shelter in the station. Eight people were crushed to death and many were injured on a staircase leading to the platform. The old station has been demolished and replaced by a characterless, box-like building.

Roll up! Roll up! The circus comes to Hampstead. Bank Holiday fairground buskers entice the customers in 1905. Right: "Harries and Harriets" pose for the camera on the Heath, 1903.

Left: The lull before the
storm on Easter Sunday
morning, 1904.

Right:
All the fun of the fair! Bank
Holiday crowds on the Heath
pass by the front of an early
cinema show—Wilson's
Living Pictures. Wilson's
bioscope show on the right is
a "ground booth—only one
penny to see the latest
animated pictures". This
bioscope was also described
as "The Electric Theatre—
where you see all the latest
life-size moving pictures.
Moral and refined. Pleasing
to ladies, gentlemen and
children."

For almost two decades from
1896 until the beginning of
World War 1, the bioscope
shared the fairground with
the organs and roundabouts.
In simple "ground booths" or
elaborate walk-up shows with
seats for 1,000, crowds
flocked to see the latest
flickering animated pictures.

Left: The rush hour in 1905! Five working horses cool off in the Whitestone pond after pulling their trade carts up the hill. Below, left: Three sad-eyed donkeys wait by the pond to give rides to Edwardian children. Donkey rides are still given there today.
Below: Jack Straw's Castle on left, with everyone dressed in their Sunday best, c. 1905.

Church Parade and Jack Straw's Castle, Hampstead

Above: The Spaniards Inn from Hampstead Lane. Above, right: The view looking down Hampstead Lane from the Spaniards, c. 1905, showing Dick Turpin House, which was demolished in 1934. The highwayman was reputed to have stayed here and stabled his horse. Right: Famed in a popular comic song—The Bull and Bush, North End, as it was in 1905.

The Vale of Health.
Above, left: Looking across
the pond towards the old
Vale of Health Hotel, 1903.
Above, right: Tea on the
hotel terrace. The two
gentlemen are enjoying a pot
of tea, price 3d, and possibly
a plate of ham for 4d. Left:
Fairground at the Vale of
Health in the period between
the wars.

Fishing in the Vale of Health pond, Edwardian style, 1903. Inset: Fishing in the 1980's. The hotel was demolished in June 1964. It was replaced by a block of flats, Spencer House (see inset) in 1967.

The Vale of Health Hotel, built in the mid-19th century, was strongly criticised by William Howitt in his book, The Northern Heights of London: "Recent times have seen Sunday dissipation reasserting itself, by the erection of a monster public house with a lofty tower and flag, to attract the attention of Sunday strollers on the Heath. Of all places, this raised its Tower of Babel bulk in that formerly quiet and favourite spot, the Vale of Health."

Platts Lane, 1905.

Frognal Lane, 1907.

The swimming baths, Finchley Road, c. 1905. The baths, near the junction with Fairfax Road, opened in 1887 and were destroyed by fire in 1972. Sainsbury's shop now occupies this site.

West Hampstead, c. 1905
Left: West End Lane, looking towards the Green and Fortune Green
Road. Above: As it is today.

Right: The opposite view from Fortune Green Road, with West End
Green on the left. Below: As it is today.

BIGGS BROS., BUTCHERS AND GRAZIERS,
274, WEST END LANE, N.W.
TELEPHONE 286 HAMPSTEAD.   FARM AT ELSTREE.

Above: Railway Hotel, West End Lane, 1903. Below, left: The old West Hampstead Library in Westbere Road, 1903. This opened in 1900 and was destroyed by a bomb during World War II. The new library in Dennington Park Road opened in 1954. Below: The Church of St. James, West Hampstead, on the corner of West End Lane and Sherriff Road. The church, built in 1887, was designed by Sir Arthur Blomfield, one of the most prolific Victorian church architects. Photo: 1904.

Finchley Road & Frognal Station, c. 1904.

WEST HAMPSTEAD. — WEST END LANE.

Above, left: Finchley Road & Frognal Station, c. 1904. This station opened on January 2, 1860, as Finchley Road (St. Johns Wood). It was renamed on October 1, 1880. See today's view above.

Left: West End Lane, with West Hampstead Station on the left, c. 1905. The Metropolitan Railway opened this station on June 30, 1879. The Bakerloo line started on November 20, 1939. In 1979 it became part of the new Jubilee line. Below: As it is today.

HAMPSTEAD. THE PUBLIC LIBRARY.

Finchley Road, Hampstead Public Library, 1905. This building on the corner of Arkwright Road dates from 1897. It was replaced by the new library at Swiss Cottage in 1964. The old library was officially opened as an Arts Centre in 1966. Inset: As it is today.

Left: Belsize Road, near the junction with Abbey Road, 1906. The large building on the right was the Princess of Wales public house, demolished in 1972. It was replaced in 1975 by the Lillie Langtry and a large block of flats, see modern picture below.

Right: Swiss Cottage Station, on the corner of Swiss Terrace, Belsize Road, right, and the Finchley Road, 1906. The old station on the Metropolitan line was built in 1868 and closed officially on August 18, 1940. A new station—below surface—on the Bakerloo line opened on November 20, 1939. This was transferred to the Jubilee line in 1979. Above: As is it today.

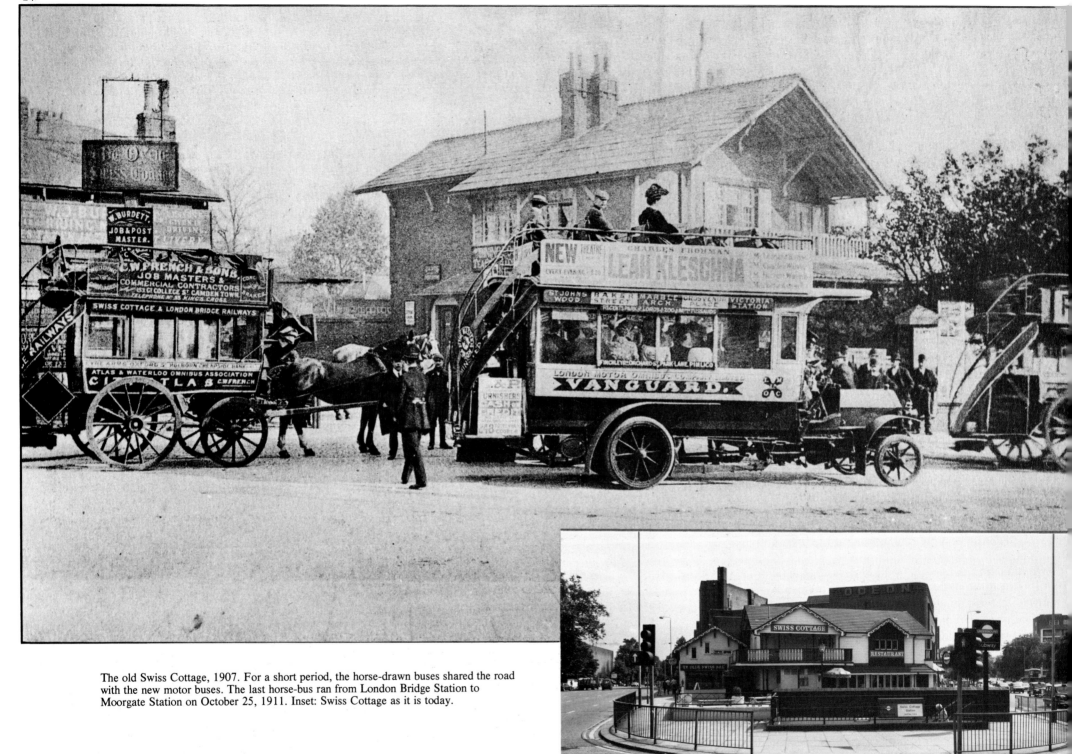

The old Swiss Cottage, 1907. For a short period, the horse-drawn buses shared the road with the new motor buses. The last horse-bus ran from London Bridge Station to Moorgate Station on October 25, 1911. Inset: Swiss Cottage as it is today.

Finchley Road, Swiss Cottage, looking towards College Crescent, in the 1920's. See modern picture, inset.

Goldhurst Terrace, from Fairhazel Gardens, 1903.

Below: Loudoun Road Station in 1904. Opened on June 2, 1889, it was renamed South Hampstead on July 10, 1922. The old station has been replaced by a modern building, see photograph above.

Steeles Road, at the junction with Fellows Road, 1904.

Adelaide Road, 1905.

Left: Maitland Park Road, 1904. The Congregational Church was destroyed by a bomb during World War II. Above: Adamson Road, 1906.

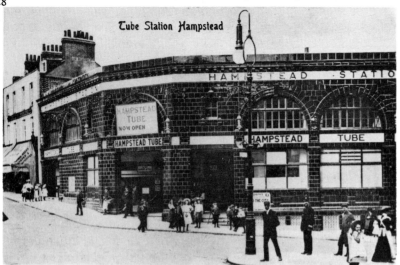

Tube Station Hampstead

Above, left: Hampstead Tube Station. Above: Belsize Park Station, shortly after the line opened in 1907. See poster, below, advertising the opening of the Hampstead Tube. The new Tube line from Charing Cross (Strand) to Golders Green was opened on June 22, 1907, when the first train was started by David Lloyd George, M.P., then President of the Board of Trade.

Left: The old Hampstead Town Hall on Haverstock Hill, 1902. It was built in 1877. The council's Engineering and Works Departments are now housed here.

Chalk Farm Road, near Camden Lock, looking towards Hampstead, 1905. Inset: The road today, now one way and minus the centre island. It is interesting to note the name Edwards can still be seen above the advertising billboard.

Queens Crescent, Haverstock Hill N.W.

Photo: 1904.

Freemasons Arms, Downshire Hill, 1905.

Kings College Road South Hampstead N.W.

Photo: 1905.

West Hampstead Fire Station, West End Lane, 1904.